AF413172

Random House Studio
An imprint of Random House Children's Books
A division of Penguin Random House LLC
1745 Broadway, New York, NY 10019
penguinrandomhouse.com
rhcbooks.com

Text copyright © 2026 by Melissa Stewart
Jacket art and interior illustrations copyright © 2026 by Becca Stadtlander

Penguin Random House values and supports copyright. Copyright fuels creativity, encourages diverse voices, promotes free speech, and creates a vibrant culture. Thank you for buying an authorized edition of this book and for complying with copyright laws by not reproducing, scanning, or distributing any part of it in any form without permission. You are supporting writers and allowing Penguin Random House to continue to publish books for every reader. Please note that no part of this book may be used or reproduced in any manner for the purpose of training artificial intelligence technologies or systems.

Random House Studio with colophon is a registered trademark of Penguin Random House LLC.

Library of Congress Cataloging-in-Publication Data is available upon request.
ISBN 978-0-593-90471-8 (trade)—ISBN 978-0-593-90472-5 (lib. bdg.)—ISBN 978-0-593-90473-2 (ebook)

The text of this book is set in 12-point Calluna.
The illustrations were rendered in gouache.
Design by Rachael Cole

Manufactured in China
10 9 8 7 6 5 4 3 2 1

The authorized representative in the EU for product safety and compliance is Penguin Random House Ireland, Morrison Chambers, 32 Nassau Street, Dublin D02 YH68, Ireland, https://eu-contact.penguin.ie.

Random House Children's Books supports the First Amendment and celebrates the right to read.

SHARKS IN KANSAS

THE ANCIENT SEA IN THE MIDDLE OF AMERICA

BY **MELISSA STEWART** ILLUSTRATED BY **BECCA STADTLANDER**

RANDOM HOUSE STUDIO · NEW YORK

KANSAS

Sharks in Kansas? Seems impossible, right?

After all, Kansas is smack-dab in the middle of
the United States—more than 1,000 miles (1,600 km)
from the closest ocean. It's home to . . .

seven million acres of wheat,

five million acres of corn,

more than six million cattle, and

almost two million pigs.

That's exactly what you'd expect in a state that's
almost 90 percent farmland.

But the world hasn't always looked the way it does today. Over time, the land beneath our feet has changed in astonishing ways.

How do we know? Fossils—and the rock around them—tell us the tale
of our planet's past and the creatures that once lived where we live now.
Our story begins 85 million years ago.

Back then, the place we now call Kansas looked like this.
Nothing but ocean stretching in every direction.

What lived in this watery world? Let's take a look.

On a typical afternoon along the coast of the Western Interior Seaway, a small herd of *Claosaurus* strolls along the beach. Above them, a *Pteranodon* glides across the sky in search of fish.

Just offshore, a hungry *Squalicorax* lurks below the water's surface. It's hoping a *Claosaurus* wades into the water.

CLAOSAURUS

Say: klay-uh-SORE-us

Class: Reptile

Group: Dinosaur

Size: 12 feet (4 m) long

Weight: 400 pounds (181 kg)

Diet: Plants

Predators: Tyrannosaurs, *Deinosuchus*

PTERANODON

Say: tuh-RAN-uh-don

Class: Reptile

Group: Pterosaur

Size: 21-foot (6 m) wingspan

Weight: 110 pounds (50 kg)

Prey: Fish

Predators: Plesiosaurs, mosasaurs,
possibly dinosaurs

SQUALICORAX

Say: skwa-lih-CORE-ax

Class: Fish

Group: Shark

Size: Up to 10 feet (3 m) long

Weight: Up to 1,000 pounds (454 kg)

Prey: Fish, turtles, mosasaurs, dinosaurs

Predators: Larger sharks, mosasaurs

HESPERORNIS

Say: hess-puh-ROR-niss

Class: Bird

Group: Seabird

Size: 5.9 feet (1.8 m) long

Weight: 20 pounds (9 kg)

Prey: Fish

Predators: Sharks, plesiosaurs,
   mosasaurs, dinosaurs

CLIDASTES

Say: KLIE-dass-teez

Class: Reptile

Group: Mosasaur

Size: 6 to 13 feet (2 to 4 m) long

Weight: Unknown

Prey: Fish, ammonites

Predators: Sharks, larger mosasaurs

SCAPANORHYNCHUS

Say: ska-pan-uh-RINK-us

Class: Fish

Group: Shark

Size: 13 feet (4 m) long

Weight: 440 pounds (200 kg)

Prey: Fish, turtles, seabirds

Predators: Larger sharks, mosasaurs

Farther out to sea, a *Hesperornis* unfolds its tiny wings and spreads them in the sun. As the flightless bird warms its body, it watches a small *Clidastes* nab a fish and cruise out of sight.

By the time *Hesperornis* notices the fearsome fin headed its way, it's too late. The *Scapanorhynchus* lunges toward its target and attacks.

STYXOSAURUS

Say: sticks-uh-SORE-us

Class: Reptile

Group: Plesiosaur

Size: Up to 39 feet (12 m) long

Weight: 5,000 pounds (2,268 kg)

Prey: Fish, squid

Predators: Mosasaurs, sharks

TYLOSAURUS

Say: tie-luh-SORE-us

Class: Reptile

Group: Mosasaur

Size: 46 feet (14 m) long

Weight: 12,000 pounds (5,443 kg)

Prey: Smaller sharks, smaller mosasaurs

Predators: *Cretoxyrhina*, other mosasaurs

XIPHACTINUS

Say: zih-FAK-tih-nus

Class: Fish

Group: Bony fish

Size: 17 feet (5 m) long

Weight: 4,000 pounds (1,814 kg)

Prey: Smaller fish

Predators: Sharks, mosasaurs

Beneath the waves, the salty sea teems with life.

ENCHODUS
Say: EN-kuh-dus
Class: Fish
Group: Bony fish
Size: 5 feet (1.5 m) long
Weight: Unknown
Prey: Smaller fish
Predators: Sharks, mosasaurs, plesiosaurs, seabirds

HOPLOSCAPHITES
Say: hop-loh-skuh-FITE-eez
Class: Mollusk
Group: Ammonite
Size: Varies
Weight: Varies
Prey: Unknown, probably small sea creatures
Predators: Sharks, *Archelon*, mosasaurs

BACULITES
Say: bak-yuh-LITE-eez
Class: Mollusk
Group: Ammonite
Size: 3 inches to 6 feet (8 cm to 2 m) long
Weight: Unknown
Prey: Zooplankton
Predators: Sharks, *Archelon*, mosasaurs

When a super-sized shark arrives on the scene, most of the sea life scatters . . .

CRETOXYRHINA
Say: kruh-tox-ee-RIE-nuh
Class: Fish
Group: Shark
Size: 26 feet (8 m) long
Weight: 10,000 pounds (4,536 kg)
Prey: Fish, mosasaurs,
    plesiosaurs, pterosaurs
Predators: Tylosaurus

. . . but not the *Tylosaurus*. The mighty mosasaur is ready for a fight.

   Tylosaurus snaps its powerful tail and races toward the intruder. But the speedy shark darts out of the way. Then it circles around, rams the reptile, and slices open the bigger beast with its razor-sharp teeth.

   The wounded *Tylosaurus* dives toward the seafloor to escape.

At the bottom of the seaway, a *Globidens* and a *Ptychodus* gorge on clams bigger than wheelbarrows with their shell-crushing teeth.

But these magnificent creatures—and the seaway they depend on—don't last forever.

GLOBIDENS

Say: GLAW-bih-denz
Class: Reptile
Group: Mosasaur
Size: 20 feet (6 m) long
Weight: 1,100 pounds (499 kg)
Prey: Small sea turtles, ammonites, clams, oysters
Predators: Sharks, larger mosasaurs

PTYCHODUS

Say: tie-KO-dus
Class: Fish
Group: Shark
Size: 33 feet (10 m) long
Weight: Up to 2,000 pounds (907 kg)
Prey: Clams, oysters, ammonites
Predators: Other sharks

PLATYCERAMUS

Say: PLAH-tee-SEER-uh-mus
Class: Mollusk
Group: Clam
Size: 3 to 9 feet (1 to 3 m) across
Weight: Unknown
Prey: Tiny sea creatures
Predators: *Globidens*, *Ptychodus*, sea turtles

As time passes, the center of North America begins to rise, and small, scattered islands appear above the water's surface. Eventually, a land bridge forms in what's now Texas, and many animals swim north.

Some creatures struggle to survive in the cooler water, but others thrive. *Archelon*—a sea turtle the size of a small car—catches ammonites with its giant jaws, while *Cretalamna* feeds on fish.

ARCHELON

Say: ARK-uh-lon
Class: Reptile
Group: Turtle
Size: 13 feet (4 m) long
Weight: 4,800 pounds (2,177 kg)
Prey: Fish, jellyfish, squid, ammonites, sponges
Predators: Sharks, mosasaurs

JELETZKYTES

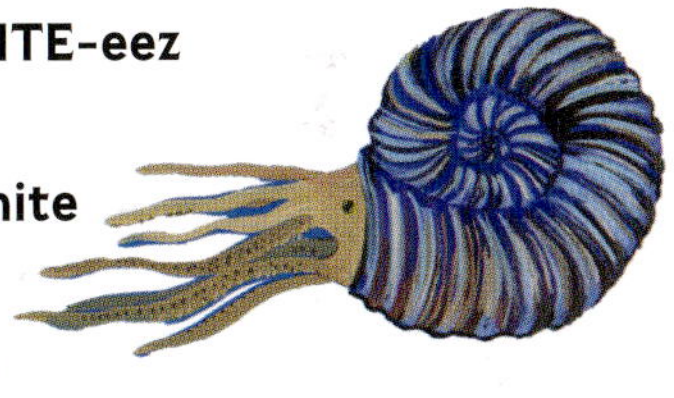

Say: JEL-ets-KITE-eez
Class: Mollusk
Group: Ammonite
Size: Varies
Weight: Varies
Prey: Small fish, clams, smaller ammonites, plankton
Predators: Sharks, *Archelon*, mosasaurs

CRETALAMNA

Say: kree-tuh-LAM-nuh
Class: Fish
Group: Shark
Size: Up to 11 feet (3.6 m) long
Weight: Unknown
Prey: Fish, turtles, squid, plesiosaurs
Predators: Larger sharks, mosasaurs

Over millions of years, the water slowly drains away.
Some creatures escape by swimming out into the Arctic
Ocean, but most aren't so lucky. As the seaway disappears,
so do untold numbers of sharks, mosasaurs, plesiosaurs,
and other living things.

Today, the Western Interior Seaway is long gone.
But signs of it still exist. And in a few places,
the evidence is right on Earth's surface.

At Dinosaur Ridge in Colorado, visitors reach
out and touch rippled sandstone that shows the
ancient sea's shoreline.

In Kansas, people walk among chalky white bluffs as tall as a seven-story building. Monument Rocks formed over millions of years as the shells of teeny-tiny seaway creatures slowly stacked up. How many coccolithophore fossils make up these stunning structures? More than anyone could possibly count.

Magnified view of a coccolithophore

HOW MONUMENT ROCKS FORMED

1. When tiny coccolithophores living in the seaway died, they sank to the seafloor. Their soft body parts rotted away, but their hard shells piled up over time.
2. For millions of years, the weight of the top layers pressed down on the lower layers. The shells stuck together and formed chalky limestone rock.
3. When the seaway dried up, wind and water gradually eroded the land surrounding the limestone. Today we see towering bluffs that rise above the plains.

In thirteen states and five Canadian provinces, fossil hunters have unearthed thousands of ancient seaway animals. Sharks. Mosasaurs. Giant clams and turtles. And that's just the beginning! They've found treasure troves of smaller creatures too.

By digging them up and studying them closely, we can peek into the past and know what the world was like when sharks swam in Kansas.

THE RISE AND FALL OF THE WESTERN INTERIOR SEAWAY

LAYERS OF EARTH

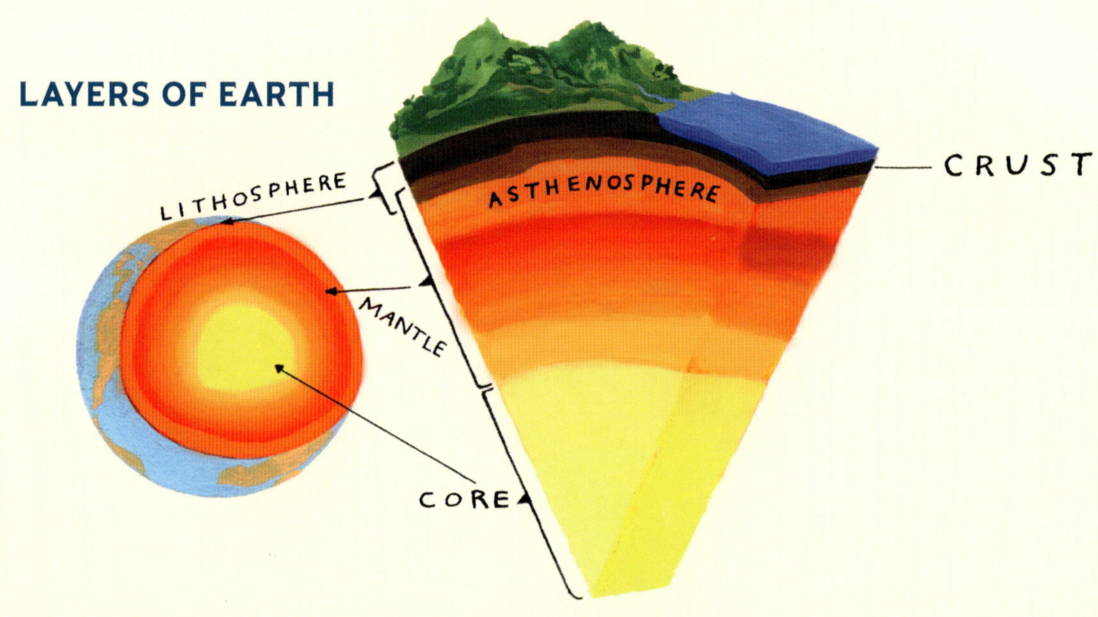

EARTH'S PLATES TODAY

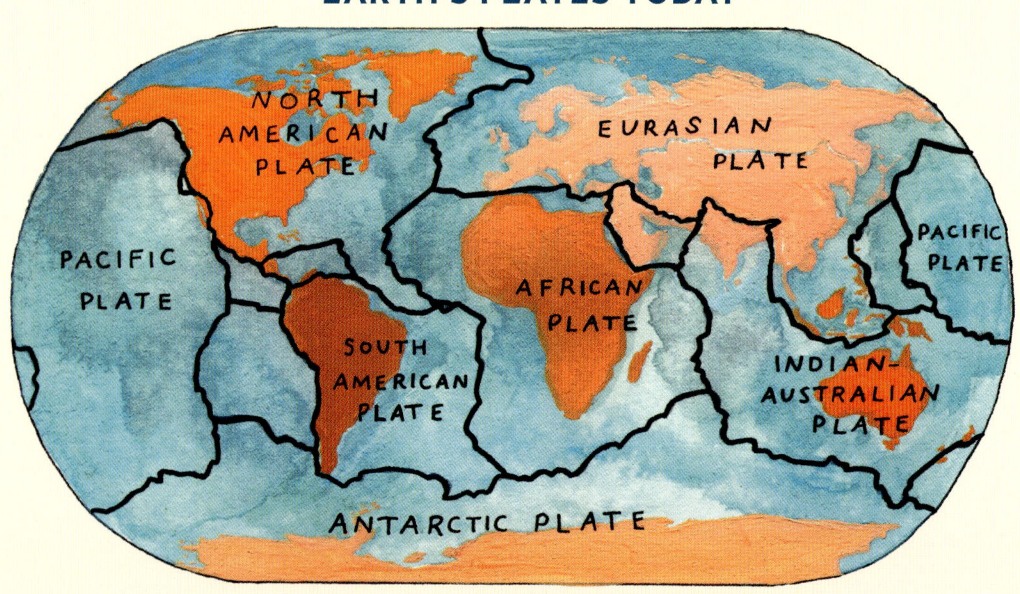

LAND ON THE MOVE

Earth has three layers—the crust, the mantle, and the core. The crust and upper mantle are made of solid rock. Together, they are called the lithosphere.

Earth's lithosphere is broken into large pieces, called plates, that fit together like a jigsaw puzzle. These hard, solid plates float on top of a hot, soft layer called the asthenosphere. Over time, this process reshapes the land and moves the continents from place to place.

Millions of years ago, Earth's floating landmasses were in very different places. And they're still on the move today.

WESTERN INTERIOR SEAWAY BASIN FORMING

SEAFLOOR SPREADING

BUMP AND SLIDE

About 160 million years ago, the Farallon Plate crashed into the North American Plate and began sliding below it. As the lithosphere bent upward, land rose in the West, and a shallow basin formed in what's now the Great Plains. Then the Farallon Plate began tugging downward on the lithosphere, and the basin grew deeper.

WHERE'D THE WATER COME FROM?

During this period, the world was much warmer than it is today. The ice caps at the North and South Poles melted, causing sea levels to rise all over the planet.

Meanwhile, plates on the ocean floor were pulling apart. During this seafloor spreading, lava oozed out of cracks in the lithosphere, then cooled and hardened to form underwater mountains. As these seamounts grew taller and wider, sea levels rose even higher.

About 130 million years ago, water from the Arctic Ocean began gushing onto land and filling the basin. By 95 million years ago, the Western Interior Seaway stretched to the Gulf of Mexico.

GOING, GOING, GONE

About 80 million years ago, the center of North America began to rise back up.

Over time, water drained into rivers, streams, and the Arctic Ocean. By 60 million years ago, the seaway had disappeared.

Selected Sources

Brosius, Liz, Jim McCauley, Bob Sawin, and Rex Buchanan. *Geology and Paleontology of Northwestern Kansas: Public Field Trip.* Kansas Geological Survey, University of Kansas, 2003.

Chang, Ching, and Lijun Liu. "Investigating the Formation of the Cretaceous Western Interior Seaway Using Landscape Evolution Simulations." *Geological Society of America Bulletin,* 2021.

"Cretaceous Atlas of Ancient Life." Digital Atlas of Ancient Life. cretaceousatlas.org.

"Dinosaur-Era Shark Fossil Discovered in Kansas; Researchers Name It Cretodus houghtonorum." DePaul University Newsroom, November 18, 2019. resources.depaul.edu/newsroom/news/press-releases/Pages/Cretodus_houghtonorum.aspx.

Dvorak, John. *How the Mountains Grew: A New Geological History of North America.* Pegasus Books, 2021.

"Episode 71: The Western Interior Seaway." *The Common Descent Podcast.* commondescentpodcast.com/2019/10/05/episode-71-the-western-interior-seaway.

Goodrich, David. *A Voyage Across an Ancient Ocean: A Bicycle Journey Through the Northern Dominion of Oil.* Pegasus Books, 2020.

Knoll, Andrew H. *A Brief History of Earth: Four Billion Years in Eight Chapters.* Custom House/HarperCollins, 2021.

Miall, Andrew D., ed. *The Sedimentary Basins of the United States and Canada,* second edition. Elsevier, 2019.

Myers, Corinne, and Bruce S. Lieberman. "Sharks That Pass in the Night: Using Geographical Information Systems to Investigate Competition in the Cretaceous Western Interior Seaway." *Proceedings of the Royal Society B,* March 7, 2011.

Prehistoric Life: The Definitive Visual History of Life on Earth. Dorling Kindersley, 2012.

Richardson, Hazel. *Dinosaurs and Prehistoric Life.* Dorling Kindersley, 2003.

Shimada, Kenshu, and Michael J. Everhart. "A New Large Late Cretaceous Lamniform Shark from North America, with Comments on the Taxonomy, Paleoecology, and Evolution of the Genus *Cretodus.*" *Journal of Vertebrate Paleontology* 39:4, November 18, 2019. DOI: 10.1080/02724634.2019.1673399.

Slattery, Joshua, William Cobban, Kevin McKinney, Peter Harries, and Ashley Sandness. "Early Cretaceous to Paleocene Paleogeography of the Western Interior Seaway: The Interaction of Eustasy and Tectonism." Wyoming Geological Association, 68th Annual Field Conference at Casper, Wyoming, June 2013.

For Further Exploration

Dinosaur! Dinosaurs and Other Amazing Prehistoric Creatures as You've Never Seen Them Before. Dorling Kindersley, 2014.

Dinosaur Ridge Virtual Experience. dinoridge.org/programs-and-events/virtual-experience.

Kunhl, Jackson. "What's That Weird Shell?" *Dig,* May–June 2014.

Stewart, Melissa. *Mega-Predators of the Past.* Peachtree, 2022.

Acknowledgments

We are grateful to the following scientists for sharing their time, expertise, and enthusiasm for the Western Interior Seaway and its inhabitants with us:

- Emily L. Bamforth, Philip J. Currie Dinosaur Museum, Wembley, Alberta, Canada

- Steve Brusatte, School of GeoSciences, University of Edinburgh, Scotland

- Andy Connolly, Kansas Geological Survey, Lawrence, Kansas

- Femke Holwerda, Royal Tyrrell Museum of Paleontology, Drumheller, Alberta, Canada

- Erin LaCount, Dinosaur Ridge, Morrison, Colorado

- David Moscato, Gray Fossil Site & Museum, East Tennessee State University, Gray, Tennessee

And a special shout-out to Laura E. Wilson, Sternberg Museum of Natural History, Fort Hays State University, Hays, Kansas, for reviewing the manuscript multiple times and answering about 1,001 questions.